Daniel Fast

The Ultimate Guide to Slow Cooker Meals for Breakfast, Lunch, and Dinner for 2016

Author: Rebecca Lacey

Table of Contents

Introduction

The Daniel Fast was initially a 10 day fast wherein water, fruits and vegetables are eaten. Apparently, the men who partook of the "sinful" food ate wheat, meat and drank the wine. It was believed in Judah that Babylonian men killed people who did not worship their false gods. In the context of the original Biblical Book as narrated by Daniel, 21 days is required to cleanse one's body and soul through fasting or a period when one mourns from the committed sins.

The Daniel Fast has been in the healthy alternative pipeline since the days of the Old Testament. The diet was first started in Babylon when a young man named Daniel was deported there together with three of his friends. Hannaih, Daniel, Azariah and Mishael were summoned for education and military training, which Christians refer to as the "Nebuchadnezzar brainwash" in 605 BC.

The group did not want to partake in food prepared for trainees and prayed to God to lead them to their righteous ways. Soon after, it was a Babylonian guard who allowed the men to eat what was just and right. Hence, a different feast was prepared for them with a promise to compare them with other men their age at the end of their training.

The Daniel Fast is a 21 day diet that prohibits the consumption of food aside from vegetables, water, and fruits, among others. While it is still considered as a method of fasting in the Christian belief, it is also considered as a method to lose weight and be strong. The usual food items are replaced by whole plant foods.

Good luck on your Daniel Fast journey. All you have to do is have faith in the Lord God. With Him, all things are possible.

Don't forget to like us on Facebook by clicking here:

http://bit.ly/1Wa1bfd

or find us by typing in "Daniel Fast Slow Cooker Meals"!

Chapter 1. Daniel Fast Shopping List

You must always remember that the line between allowed and forbidden is quite thin for the Daniel Fast diet. Just take salt as an example. Iodized, rock or other salty additives to food are banned in this diet. However, you may use the Himalayan salt during the Daniel Fast. This kind of salt has natural elements that are known to regulate water in the body. It also promotes the pH level of the cells among other things.

In the Old Testament, Adam and Eve were advised not to eat the forbidden fruit. The Daniel Fast allows this fruit but it does not agree with the consumption of dairy, sugar, meat, bread, oil, alcohol and coffee. Eggs and yeast are also included in the foods to avoid.

Patience and determination is needed to succeed in a Daniel Fast diet. It is now time to say goodbye to the sinful foods that you have grown up with. For a stronger and healthier you, here is your guide to bring with when you go to the grocery store to buy the ingredients for your 21 day menu. Keep in mind that you are not to buy everything right away since it is your option to choose the right kind of meals within the Daniel Fast that you will prepare for a certain day.

Vegetables (all kinds in frozen, cooked or raw form)
Fruits (all kinds in cooked, fresh, dried or frozen form)
Drinks

> Water
> Coconut water
> Almond milk
> Vegetable juice
> Coconut kefir

Legumes and Beans (all kinds that are cooked and dried)

Seeds and Nuts (all kinds that are dry roasted, raw or sprouted) *unsalted

Whole grain (flour, bread or wheat is not permitted)

> Millet
> Buckwheat
> Quinoa
> Barley
> Brown rice
> Sourdough (this is the only bread allowed)
> Whole grain pasta (allowed but not liberally consumed)

Chapter 2. Daniel Fast Benefits and Frequently Asked Questions

It is clear that there are several benefits you can receive from the Daniel Fast but at the end of the day, you need to know that it should begin with being motivated spiritually. It is chronicled in the Bible, in Isaiah 58:6, that when you "loose the bonds of wickedness" your soul shall be set free. That is why this diet will provide your body with the following:

- Addiction to meat, dairy and sugar is lessened
- Anxiety is lessened
- Brain fog is decreased
- High cholesterol levels are decreased
- Depression and lethargy is lessened
- Gradual weight loss is promoted
- Energy levels are increased
- Toxins in the body are eliminated
- Hormonal levels are normalized
- Skin conditions are normalized

In starting the Daniel Fast, it is always advised by physicians to get tested for ailments that may interfere should it interact with certain medications. If you are a woman, it is necessary to check if you are pregnant or nursing. If you are on a special diet that requires you to consume food that is high in protein and carbohydrates, then the Daniel Fast is not for you.

In the event you are not in the red flag category as stated above, then congratulations! The Daniel Fast is the perfect diet for you to consider. By now, you have a lot of questions running through your mind. Majority of the dieters who would want to try the Daniel Fast have asked similar questions like you do right now.

For your reference, here are the most frequently asked questions.

FAQ #1: Meat is not allowed in this diet so where can I source my protein requirements?

Worry not that the Daniel Fast prohibits the consumption of meat in your diet. There are other sources of food that have the same or even higher levels of protein! Do eat lentils, brown rice, quinoa and almonds. You can still receive your dose of protein from these food items.

FAQ #2: During my fasting, am I stuck with eating the food I prepare at home? Does it mean I cannot dine in restaurants anymore?

Try not to associate fasting as if it were the end of the world. With the Daniel Fast, you may eat at your favorite restaurants for as long as you specifically order plain baked potatoes. When it comes to salad, go ahead and indulge; you are allowed to eat them for as long as they are dressed in olive oil.

FAQ #3: I cannot live without bread! You mean to say this fasting is made up of just fruits and plants?

You need to understand that the Daniel Fast started more than 2,000 years ago. This means that grains were only limited to a handful species. Right now, you may consider the sourdough bread.

FAQ #4: What are the Daniel Fast guidelines I have to follow? Are they super strict that I faint with thirst and hunger?

The Daniel Fast is not at all depriving you from living, so do not get so paranoid. This way of fasting is all about denying yourself of the food you have immensely consumed in the past. When you feel hungry, stop for a while and put yourself in the presence of the Lord. Praying and focusing on the word of God will give you enlightenment on the right things to do in life. The Do's and Don'ts of eating are guides for you to follow in order to achieve the results you are aiming for.

FAQ #5: Can I eat seafood while on the Daniel Fast?

No. Mussels from shells, shrimps and fish are considered as meat. The Daniel Fast is this generation's contribution to the Christian faith that complies with the morals of vegetarianism in order to strengthen one's mind and body.

Looking back, the same morals were prominent in abstaining from eating meat as stated in Daniel 10:1-2 *"In those days I, Daniel, was mourning three full weeks. [I ate] No pleasant food, no meat or wine came into my mouth; nor did I anoint myself at all, until three whole weeks were fulfilled."*

You can still feel stronger and full when you eat soy-based food. They are allowed in the Daniel Fast. If at first you fail, just keep praying for strength and in a couple of days, you shall prevail.

Chapter 3. 10-Day Daniel Fast Diet Plan

The following is a diet plan that you can follow for 10 days. Prepare a combination of breakfast-lunch-dinner recipes of your choice for the rest of the 21-day Daniel Fast, or for as long as you want to stay in the diet.

Day 1

Breakfast: Slow Cooked Tofu and Celery Squares

Ingredients
8 slices whole grain bread
1 block soft tofu
2 small celery stalks
2 tbsp. fresh parsley (chopped)
1 pinch of Himalayan salt and black pepper
8 tomatoes (thickly sliced)
8 small lettuce leaves
2 scallions

Directions
- In a medium-sized bowl, stir in scallions, Himalayan salt, celery, and pepper; set aside.
- Place the soft tofu on a circular pan and place at the bottom of the metallic slow cooker base.
- To cook, set the heat on low for 4 hours.
- Top the tofu with tomato slices and lettuce.

Lunch: Slow cooked Chipotle and Pinto Beans

Ingredients

    2 cans tomatoes (diced)
    2 tbsp. extra virgin olive oil
    3 onions (diced)
    8 cloves garlic (minced)
    1/4 cup chili powder
    2 tbsp. ground cumin
    Himalayan salt (to taste)
    4 cans pinto beans
    2 tbsp. chipotle in adobo sauce (minced)
    2 cups corn kernels

Directions

- In a blender, add all the diced tomatoes and set to a pulse for 30 seconds.
- In a skillet, sauté the garlic, ground cumin, onions, Himalayan salt, and chili powder for 15 minutes.
- In a slow cooker, pour the tomato mixture together with the chipotles and beans.
- Close the lid and set to cook for 7 hours on low heat or 5 hours on high.
- The cooked corn kernels are mixed with the chili soup before serving.

Dinner: Slow Cooked Pinto and Red Kidney Bean Paella with Jalapeño

Ingredients

> 3 tbsp. olive oil
> 1 cup onion (finely chopped)
> 1 cup brown rice
> 1 cup corn kernels
> 2 garlic cloves
> 1 and ½ cups pinto beans
> 2 tbsp. red bell peppers (finely diced)
> 1 can of red kidney beans
> 1 can of chickpeas
> 1 can of stewed tomatoes (include the juice)
> 1 cup zucchini
> Himalayan salt (to taste)
> ¼ cup cilantro leaves
> 2 tsp. jalapeño pepper
> 1 tsp. ground cumin
> 11/2 cups vegetable broth

Directions

- In a small pan, sauté the chopped onions until they turn golden.
- In a slow cooker, add the ground cumin, rice and garlic, dried tomatoes, and stewed tomatoes.
- Mix in the chickpeas, red kidney beans, corn kernels, Himalayan salt, and zucchini.
- Set the timer for 10 minutes on high heat.
- Once done, plate the rice and beans in bowls; garnish with bell peppers, cilantro and jalapeño.

Day 2

Breakfast: No Hurry Potato Casserole

Ingredients
    2 celery stalks
    1 carrot
    1/4 cup water
    1 pinch ground cinnamon
    1 onion
    1/2 tsp. Himalayan salt
    1 green bell pepper
    2 potatoes
    1 pinch ground cloves
    1 tbsp. olive oil
    1/2 tbsp. paprika
    1/4 tsp. red pepper (crushed)
    Cooking spray (for greasing)
    1 tsp. black pepper

Directions
- In a slow cooker, add olive oil, onions, celery, green pepper and carrots until they soften.
- Add black pepper, cinnamon, paprika, salt and garlic.
- Prepare the casserole dish and layer the potato slices at the bottom.
- Once the potatoes have covered the entire pan, add the vegetables mixture.
- Cover the circular glass casserole dish cook on low for 2 hours.
- Serve on a plate and enjoy your meal!

Lunch: Corn and Black Beans with Salsa

Ingredients

    1 bag corn (frozen)
    2 cups cooked black beans
    4 red bell peppers (organic)
    2 tbsp. olive oil
    2 avocados
    1 cup brown rice
    2 cups plain salsa
    4 green peppers
    2 cups water
    1 tbsp. chili powder
    1 red onion
    2 cups eggplants (diced)
    Himalayan salt and pepper (to taste)

Directions

- In a medium-sized pot, add water and the brown rice; cook for 50 minutes.
- In a separate bowl, add warm vinegar and soak all the peppers and eggplants.
- On a chopping board, dice the eggplants, onions and green peppers and avocado.
- In a glass dish, place the pepper halves, add olive oil and eggplants.
- In a pot, add the cooked rice, mashed avocados, seasoning, salsa, and beans.
- Place the salsa and vegetables inside large bell peppers.
- Bake it in the oven for 30 minutes at 350 degrees F.
- Serve on individual plates.

Dinner: Apricot-Glazed Chili Tofu

Ingredients

    1 jar apricot preserves
    1 jar chili sauce
    1 package soft tofu

Directions

- In a slow cooker, arrange the hard tofu.
- In a small bowl, mix the apricot preserve with the chili sauce.
- Pour the apricot-chili mixture over the hard tofu; mix with your hands to fully coat.
- Cover the lid and set heat on low; cook for 4 hours.
- Once the hard tofu is ready, pour a generous serving of the sweet and chili sauce over the chicken.
- To serve, transfer to a plate and enjoy.

Day 3

Breakfast: Porridge of Oats, Coconuts with Raisins and Dried Apples

Ingredients

>   1/2 cup raisins
>   1/2 cup sliced almonds
>   1/2 cup shredded coconut
>   1/2 cup chopped dried apples
>   2 cups rolled oats
>   3 tablespoons vegetable oil

Directions

- In a large glass dish, add the coconut, almond, vegetable oil and oats.
- In a slow cooker, set timer to 8 hours on low heat.
- When the oats are done, add the dried apples and raisins.
- Serve with a cup of soy milk and enjoy.

Lunch: Crushed Walnuts and Oats in Black Bean Burgers

Ingredients

1 tsp. ground cumin
1/2 cup walnuts
1 tbsp. flax seeds
1 tsp. paprika
1 cup almond milk
1/2 cup rolled oats
1 pinch ground cinnamon
2 cans black beans
1/2 cup cooked sweet potato

1/4 cup onion
1 chili pepper
3 cloves garlic
1 small white mushroom
1/2 tsp. soy sauce
1/2 cup vegetable oil
1 tsp. Himalayan salt
6 slices of whole grain bread

Directions

- In a slow cooker, add the sweet potatoes and black beans and set timer to 7 hours on high heat.
- Once done, release steam and pour into a blender.
- Add walnuts, flax seeds, oats, salt, paprika and cumin; process until rough.
- In a small bowl, combine the chili, mushrooms, soy sauce, almond milk, onions and garlic; add to the beans mixture.
- Lightly grease your hands with olive oil and roll the mixture into bean patties.
- In a skillet, cook the bean patties for 5 minutes per side.
- Serve the black bean burgers on whole grain bread and enjoy!

Dinner: Slow Cooked Sweet Potatoes and Flaked Coconut Pie

Ingredients

1 cup oat flour
1 teaspoon orange zest
2 lbs. sweet potatoes
¼ cup coconut flakes
¼ cup pecans (finely chopped)
½ teaspoon cinnamon
½ cup raw honey
¼ cup orange juice
1/8 teaspoon nutmeg

Directions

- In a slow cooker, place all the sweet potatoes and cook for 6 hours on low heat.
- Once it is cooked, peel the skin and mash until smooth.
- In a blender, add the orange juice, raw honey, oat flour, cinnamon, orange zest, nutmeg and sweet potatoes.
- Pour the contents into a baking dish, top with pecans, coconut flakes and bake for 20 minutes at 350 degrees F.
- Serve on individual plates, thank the Lord for the blessings and enjoy the meal.

<u>Day 4</u>

Breakfast: Hot Sticky Rice with Dates and Apples

Ingredients
- 2 cups brown rice
- 1 can of coconut milk
- 1/4 tsp. cinnamon
- 1 and ½ cups mashed bananas
- 1 cup dates (chopped)
- ¼ tsp. nutmeg
- 1 and ½ cups chopped apples
- ½ cup walnuts

Directions
- In a slow cooker, add the apples, dates, cinnamon, coconut milk, brown rice, nutmeg, and mashed bananas.
- Set timer to 2 hours on low heat.
- Once the brown rice is fluffy, sprinkle chopped walnuts on top; serve on plate to enjoy.

Lunch: Spicy Chickpea Burgers

Ingredients

3 tablespoons chickpea flour
2 cloves fresh garlic
1 cup soy milk (in lieu of 1 egg)
2 teaspoons ground coriander
1 large carrot
½ teaspoon fresh ground black pepper (to taste)
2 green onions
2 cups cooked chickpeas
½ teaspoon cayenne pepper (to taste)
1 and 1/2 teaspoons seasoning salt
2 teaspoons ground cumin
Cooking oil

Ingredients for the Topping

2 slices tomatoes
1 tablespoon pickle relish
4 rings of red onion
A dollop of mustard
1 leaf of lettuce
Whole grain burger buns or rolls

Directions

- In a food processor, add the green onions, carrot chunks and garlic; pulse until chunky.
- Add in the soy milk, chickpeas, spices and chickpea flour; pulse for 12 minutes until paste forms.
- With lightly greased hands, form the chickpea batter into patties.
- In a slow cooker, add the chickpea patties and cook for 6 hours on low heat.
- Transfer the burgers into buns and top with your choice of vegetables.
- Serve with a plate of the remaining toppings and enjoy.

Dinner: Lima, Chickpeas and Barley Soup

Ingredients
   1 cup carrots (sliced)
   1 can of baby Lima dreams (green)
   1 tbsp. olive oil
   1 ½ cups of barley (pre-cooked)
   4 tsp. thyme leaves (dried)
   1 cup onions (chopped)
   1 large potato
   ½ cup celery (sliced)
   3 minced cloves garlic
   2 bay leaves
   1 can of chickpeas
   2 tbsp. tomato paste
   1 cup spinach leaves

Directions
- In a pan, sauté the celery, onions and garlic in a pan; once the vegetables are half-way cooked, stir in herbs, coconut flour and pepper.
- Transfer celery mixture in a slow cooker.
- Add the beans, vegetable broth, tomato paste and beans.
- Next, add the carrots, potatoes, spinach leaves, bay leaves and carrots.
- Cover the slow cooker lid and set to 6 hours on low heat.
- Once cooked, remove the bay leaves and ladle soup into bowls; serve immediately.

Day 5

Breakfast: Strawberry Sourdough bread with Apricots

Ingredients
- 2 cups almond milk
- 1/8 teaspoon apple pie spice
- 1/2 teaspoon vanilla
- 8 slices Sourdough bread
- 2 tablespoons apricot spreadable fruit
- 1/2 cup strawberry
- Nonstick cooking spray

Directions
- Coat a griddle with cooking spray.
- In a small bowl, combine the apricot spreadable fruit, strawberries and apple pie spice.
- Cut the bread in the middle and fill it with the fruit mixture.
- In a separate bowl, mix the vanilla and almond milk.
- Dip the sourdough bread in vanilla-almond mixture and place the bread on a circular pan; slow cook for 2 hours on low heat.
- In small saucepan, place the remaining apricot spreadable fruit and stir it until it melts.
- Transfer onto a circular pan and bake for 10 minutes at 350 degrees F.
- Once the sourdough bread is crunchy, remove from oven and serve right away.

Lunch: Sunflower Crusted Tofu Burgers with Nuts and Spices

Ingredients

1/2 cup cashew nuts
1 lb. tofu (extra-firm)
1 tbsp. Dijon mustard
1/2 tsp. ground cayenne
1/2 cup sunflower seeds
1 tsp. ground cumin
1/2 cup sliced mushrooms
1 tbsp. soy sauce
1 tbsp. olive oil (extra-virgin)
1/4 tsp. fine Himalayan salt
Whole grain hamburger buns

Directions

- In a food processor, put all the ingredients in the list except for the olive oil.
- Pulse the mixture until chunky.
- With lightly greased olive oil, roll yours hands to create patties.
- In a slow cooker, add a tablespoon of olive oil and cook the patties for about 10 minutes.
- Slice the hamburger buns and place one cooked tofu burger.
- Serve on a plate with a handful of toasted cashew nuts and enjoy!

Dinner: Real Keeper Whole Grain Noodles

Ingredients

    2 tbsp. canola oil
    ½ lb. whole gain thin noodles
    1 cup cucumber (sliced)
    2 tbsp. lemon juice
    1 tbsp. garlic (minced)
    1.2 tsp. chili flakes
    1 tsp. sesame oil
    ½ cup fresh cilantro
    3 tbsp. soy sauce
    1 tsp. ginger (minced)
    1 tsp. peanut butter
    1 cup snow peas
    ½ tsp. red bell pepper
    ½ cup chunked pineapple
    ¼ tsp. Himalayan salt
    1/4 tsp. ground pepper

Directions

- In a pot, cook the thin noodles according to directions for about 5 minutes.
- Drain well and reserve a cup of noodle water; add canola oil to coat the noodles before setting side.
- In a slow cooker, add the soy sauce, cilantro, garlic, oil and ginger.
- Stir the contents before adding the oil, red pepper flakes and peanut butter.
- Once done, toss in the snow peas, cucumber, bell pepper and pineapple chunks; toss noodles to incorporate ingredients.
- Close slow cooker lid and cook for 2 hours in low heat.

Day 6

Breakfast: Scramblin' Curried Tofu

Ingredients
- 2 tomatoes (diced)
- 1 bunch spinach leaves
- 3 cloves garlic
- Himalayan salt and ground pepper (to taste)
- 1 tsp. curry powder
- 1 onion (diced)
- 1 block hard tofu
- 1/2 tsp. turmeric powder
- 1/2 tsp. ground cumin

Directions
- Use a large skillet to sauté the garlic and onions in oil.
- In a slow cooker, add the spinach leaves, turmeric, Himalayan salt, tofu, pepper, tomatoes and curry powder.
- Set the slow cooker for 3 hours on high heat.
- Serve the tofu omelet on a plate and enjoy your meal!

Lunch: Brunching on Potato Frittata with Scallions

Ingredients

2 potatoes (shredded)
2 blocks firm tofu (chunked)
3 tbsp. soy sauce
1 onion (chopped)
2 tsp. Himalayan salt
¼ cup olive oil
½ tsp. ground pepper
4 garlic cloves (minced)

Directions

- In a skillet, sauté the scallions and onions in oil; toss in the garlic and cook until lightly brown.
- In a slow cooker, add the remaining ingredients; cook for 5 hours on high heat.
- Once the potatoes are tender, open the lid and add the garlic mixture.
- Stir contents and close the lid to infuse the heat.
- Transfer the contents to a blender and puree until smooth.
- Ladle the potato mixture into a baking dish and bake 40 minutes at 350 degrees F.
- Once the tofu and potato frittata turn golden brown, remove from oven and serve.

Dinner: Slow Cooked Cabbage, Ginger and Apples over Brown Rice

Ingredients

    2 large apples
    1 tsp. ginger (grated)
     1/4 cup lime juice
    1/4 cup walnut oil
    2 tbsp. rice vinegar
    1/4 tsp. Himalayan salt
    4 cups cabbage (shredded)
    Ground pepper (to taste)
    1/4 tsp. celery seeds

Directions

- In a bowl, combine the lime juice, rice vinegar, walnut oil and ginger.
- Whisk the contents and slowly add the ground pepper and Himalayan salt; set aside.
- In a slow cooker, add the apples and cabbage; set heat to high to cook for 30 minutes.
- Once the apples and cabbage are soft, add in the rest of the bowl's contents.
- Serve on top of cooked brown rice and enjoy.

Day 7

Breakfast: Whole Grain Burrito in Tofu, Tomato and Onions

Ingredients

  2 cups cooked brown rice
  1 cup extra firm tofu
  4 whole grain burritos
  3 medium tomatoes
  2 tbsp. olive oil
  1 tsp. Himalayan salt
  2 cloves garlic
  2 tsp. fresh lime juice
  2 pieces of Serrano chilies
  3 cups vegetable broth
  1/2 cup white onions
  1/2 cup fresh cilantro

Directions

- In a skillet, sauté the garlic and onions in olive oil; set aside.
- In a slow cooker, add the tofu, chile, brown rice, lime juice, Himalayan salt, tomatoes, and vegetable broth.
- Set the slow cooker at 3 hours on low heat.
- Once the rice and tofu are cooked, spoon it in a burrito and wrap.
- Garnish the burrito with a lime wedge and serve.

Lunch: Zucchini, Tofu and Beet Curry

Ingredients
>   1 block firm tofu
>   1 small zucchini
>   2 scallions (chopped)
>   1 package Enoki mushrooms
>   2 tsp. curry powder
>   1 red onion
>   12 grape tomatoes
>   1 tbsp. lime juice
>   3 cloves garlic
>   2 tbsp. coconut oil
>   1 can of coconut milk
>   2 carrots
>   1 jalapeño pepper
>   2 golden beets
>   1/2 tsp. red pepper flakes
>   1/4 cup cilantro (coarsely chopped)
>   Himalayan salt and pepper (to taste)
>   Cooked rice (for serving)

Directions
- In a pan, add oil and sauté tomatoes, garlic, scallions, beets and onions.
- In a slow cooker, add carrots, firm tofu, and the rest of the ingredients.
- Cover the lid and cook for 30 minutes on high heat.
- Once done, open the lid and add the beets mixture; stir to combine.
- Grab a large serving plate and pour the contents around the cooked rice.

Dinner: Spicy Black Beans Soup in Celery and Tomatoes

Ingredients

2 cans of black beans
1 tsp. garlic (minced)
1 can tomatoes (diced)
1 tbsp. olive oil
2 tsp. jalapeño (finely chopped)
2 cup celery (finely chopped)
1 tsp. ground cumin
2 cups water
1 cup onion (finely chopped)
Himalayan salt and pepper (to taste)

Directions

- In a pan, sauté garlic and onions; add the jalapeño peppers and celery to sweat.
- In a slow cooker, add the diced tomatoes, black beans and water.
- Set to high heat and cook for 3 hours.
- Once the beans are soft, transfer the ingredients to a blender and puree.
- Remove contents from the blender and pour into a pot; heat to a rolling boil.
- Ladle the soup into individual bowls and serve.

Day 8

Breakfast: Slow Cooked Tofu

Ingredients
>   1/3 cup coconut milk
>   1 small red onion
>   2 tsp. olive oil
>   ¼ tsp. black pepper
>   1 block soft tofu
>   2 tbsp. fresh dill

Directions
- In a large skillet, add vegetable oil and sauté the onions until soft; set aside.
- In a medium-sized bowl, combine the coconut milk, and black pepper.
- Place the tofu in a slow cooker, add a cup of water to maintain moisture and set it on high for 30 minutes.
- Serve on a plate; add the tofu, and a sprinkle of dill.

Lunch: Spicy Bell Peppers in Lime and Scallions

Ingredients

- 2 jalapeño peppers
- 2 scallions
- ½ tsp. black pepper
- 2 garlic cloves
- 4 large bell peppers
- ½ tsp. ground cinnamon
- 1 tbsp. soy sauce
- 2 tbsp. lime juice
- 2 tsp. fresh thyme (chopped)
- ½ tsp. ground allspice
- 2 tsp. olive oil
- 1 tsp. hot pepper sauce
- Lime wedges (for garnishing)

Directions

- In a food processor, add the black pepper, cloves, jalapeño peppers, cinnamon, soy sauce, all spice, lime juice, thyme and hot pepper sauce.
- Puree all the ingredients and transfer the pepper mixture into a zip-lock bag.
- Shake the bag gently to allow the marinade to evenly coat bell peppers.
- Use a slow cooker to cook the bell peppers for 4 hours on low heat.
- Once done, transfer the bell peppers on a plate and squeeze one lemon wedge.
- Garnish with scallions on top and serve.

Dinner: Pepperoncini Peppers, Tofu and Garlic

Ingredients
Slivers of garlic
Jar of pepperoncini peppers
1 block of firm tofu

Directions
- Make slice slits in the peppers and insert the slivers of garlic; add ingredients in the slow cooker.
- Add the tofu and pepperoncini peppers together with its juice and cook for 40 minutes on high heat.
- Once the meat of peppers are tender, slice them and serve on a plate.

Day 9

Breakfast: Spicy Casserole on a Bed of Eggplants

Ingredients
> 8 oz. of marinara
> 1 tbsp. coconut oil
> 6 small eggplants (sliced)
> Parsley (garnishing)

Directions
- In a baking dish, transfer the eggplants to the bottom.
- Layer on the marinara sauce.
- Set the slow cooker on high heat for 30 minutes.
- Once done, serve while hot.

Lunch: Spicy Mediterranean Quinoa and Corn Basket

Ingredients

2 cups water
1 can crushed tomatoes
1 tbsp. dried parsley
1 jalapeno pepper
1 onion
1 green bell pepper
1 cup frozen corn kernels
1 tbsp. olive oil
1 tbsp. ground cumin
1 cup uncooked quinoa
4 cloves garlic
1 tbsp. chili powder
1 red bell pepper
1 zucchini
2 cans black beans
1 tsp. dried oregano leaves
Ground black pepper
Salt (to taste)
1/4 cup chopped fresh cilantro

Directions

- In a saucepan, add water and bring it to a boil for about 5 minutes.
- Mix in the quinoa and simmer for 20 minutes until it fully absorbs the water.
- Cook the firm tofu in the slow cooker for 3 hours on low heat.
- Add the olive oil, onions and jalapeno peppers around the pan.
- Add cumin and chili powder in the pot and drop the black beans, tomatoes, zucchini, parsley, oregano and the bell peppers.
- Add the vegetables and simmer the quinoa pilaf and corn kernels.
- Once the vegetables have softened, reduce the heat and use a ladle to serve the soup.
- Garnish with extra cilantro leaves.

Dinner: Pita with Hummus and Spinach

Ingredients
> 2 tbsp. olive oil
> 2 tbsp. parsley
> 1/4 small red onion
> 3/4 cup hummus (store-bought)
> Black pepper
> 1 and 1/2 tsp. dried oregano
> 1 lb. spinach
> 1 lemon
> 4 flat pitas (preferably whole grain)
> Himalayan salt (to taste)

Directions
- In a large bowl, combine the dried oregano, salt and black pepper.
- In a slow cooker, add olive oil and cook the spinach leaves for 10 minutes on high heat.
- Place the beef patty on a plate, top with onions, parsley and hummus.
- Garnish with spinach and lemon wedges.

Day 10

Brunch: Slow Cooked Tofu in Chipotle and Turnips

Ingredients
1 turnip root (cut into cubes)
1 block hard tofu
2 tbsp. coconut oil
1 diced medium onion
1/2 tsp. sage
3 cups chicken broth
1 butternut squash (diced)
1/2 tsp. basil
1/2 tsp. allspice
1 14.5 ounce can diced tomatoes
1/2 tsp. black pepper
1/2 tsp. chili pepper (ground)
1 rutabaga (cubed)
1/2 tsp. paprika

Marinade
3 chipotle peppers in adobo sauce
3 cloves garlic
1 tbsp. ground mustard
1/4 cup honey
2 tbsp. apple cider vinegar
1 tsp. chili powder
1 8 ounce can tomato sauce
1/2 tsp. Himalayan salt
1/2 tsp. black pepper

Directions:
- Blend all marinade ingredients in blender or food processor.
- Pour coconut oil in bottom of the slow cooker
- Add chopped onions and spread turnip, butternut squash and rutabaga evenly on top of onion.
- Add the rest of the ingredients, then cover and set heat on low for 4 hours until the tofu softens.
- Once done, serve on a plate and enjoy the spicy treat!

Dinner: Pita with Hummus and Spinach

Ingredients
2 tbsp. olive oil
2 tbsp. parsley
1/4 small red onion
1 large jar of hummus (store-bought)
Black pepper
1 and 1/2 tsp. dried oregano
5 lbs. spinach
1 lemon
4 flat whole grain pitas
Himalayan salt (to taste)

Directions
- In a large bowl, combine the oregano, salt and pepper.
- In a slow cooker, add olive oil and cook the spinach for 1 hour on low heat.
- Place the wilted spinach on a plate, top with onions, oregano mixture, parsley and hummus.
- Heat the pita and serve with the hummus.
-

Conclusion

Thank you again for downloading this book! At the end of this conclusion, check out the preview of my "Slow Cooking for Two" book for free!

I hope this book was able to help you to successfully complete the Daniel Fast. Did you know that by creating meals, you save time the following day? All you have to do is pop a serving or two in the microwave before you leave for work. You also save on money since you can extend the meals you have prepared for lunch as well. But the most important part of the Daniel Fast is the waiting time for food to cook may be used to be one with the Lord. The silence and tranquility is bestowed on you by the Daniel Fast.

Joel 2:12 sums it up with these words *"Now, therefore," says the Lord, "Turn to Me with all your heart, with fasting, with weeping and with mourning".* Indeed, the Daniel Fast will help you come into terms with yourself. I hope you become enlightened and determined to complete the fast.

The next step is to check out my other book: "Slow Cooking: Best Simple and Deliciously Healthy Recipes for Two", I'm sure it will help you to cook healthy and make great meals on the go!

Finally, if you enjoyed this book, then I'd like to ask you for a favor, would you be kind enough to leave a review for this book on Amazon? It'd be greatly appreciated!

Click here http://amzn.to/1U7azgb to leave a review for this book on Amazon! Don't forget to like Daniel Fast Slow Cooker Meals! LIKE US ON FACEBOOK

https://www.facebook.com/DanielFastRecipes/

To purchase the next book in this series: "Slow Cooking for Two: Best Simple and Deliciously Healthy Recipes Updated for 2016 ", click HERE http://amzn.to/1TBsMna

Thank you and good luck!

Preview Of *"Slow Cooking for Two: Best Simple and Deliciously Healthy Recipes for 2016"*

Chapter 1: Easy-to-Prep, Fresh, and Flavorful Recipes

Slow Cooking, especially for beginners, could be fun when you make use of fresh and flavorful ingredients to create easy to prepare—but definitely delicious dishes. You'll find some in this chapter.

Slow-Cooked Jambalaya

Prep: 10 minutes
Cook: 8 hours 2 minutes (low) / 3 to 4 hours (high)

Ingredients:
1 lb boneless and skinless chicken halves cut into cubes
1 can tomatoes, diced and juiced
1 lb sausage, sliced
1 cup chicken broth
1 cup celery, chopped
1 large onion, chopped
1 lb frozen shrimp, thawed and cooked without tails
½ tsp dried thyme
1 tsp cayenne pepper
2 tsp Cajun Seasoning
2 tsp dried oregano

Instructions:
Mix chicken, tomatoes, sausage, green bell pepper, celery, onion, and broth before adding thyme, cayenne pepper, Cajun seasoning, parsley, and oregano.
Cover the dish and cook accordingly. Add shrimp in the last 30 minutes of cooking time.

Slow-Cooked Chicken Stew with Gnocchi

Prep: 15 minutes
Cook: 6 to 8 hours 2 minutes (low) / 4 to 5 hours (high)

Ingredients:
5 oz fresh baby spinach
2 to 3 cloves garlic
6 slices bacon
2 1lb mini potato gnocchi
2 12 oz cans evaporated milk
2 Tbsp cornstarch dissolved in 2 Tbsp water
4 cups chicken broth
1 tsp salt
1 tsp poultry seasoning
1 to 2 tsp Italian seasoning
1 to 2 tsp dried basil
2 cups mixed carrots, celery, and onions
1 lb skinless, boneless, chicken breasts

Instructions:
In a slow cooker, add the chicken, 2 cups mixed carrots, celery, and onions, seasonings, broth, and salt. Slow-cook accordingly (refer to times stated above).

Add evaporated milk, cornstarch mixture, and gnocchi. Stir and bring the cover back.

Fry bacon until crispy and sauté with garlic for at least a minute. Add to the slow cooker and stir to combine.

Add more liquid, if desired.

Season with salt and pepper, to taste.

Slow-Cooked Cuban Pork and Black Beans

Prep: 15 minutes
Cook: 8 hours, 45 minutes

Ingredients:
¼ cup fresh cilantro, chopped
2 ¾ cups unsalted chicken stock
2 2/3 cup cooked white rice
1 jalapeno pepper, seeded and sliced thinly
1 ½ cups tomatoes, chopped
1 bay leaf
1 ½ tsp crushed red pepper
2 tsp ground cumin
2 tsp paprika
¼ cup fresh oregano, divided
10 garlic cloves, chopped and divided
2 ¼ cups chopped onion, divided
1 lb dried black beans
1 bone-in pork shoulder, trimmed
4 center cut bacon slices, chopped
1 medium orange, quartered
1 ½ tsp freshly ground black pepper
1 cup fresh orange juice
½ cup cilantro stems, chopped

Instructions:

Combine chicken stock, cilantro stems, orange juice, and medium orange in a blender, and pulse until smooth. Add salt and black pepper and then cook bacon until crisp.

Cook pork drippings for 8 minutes in medium high heat. Add pork shoulder, and uncooked black beans.

Add garlic cloves and onion and sauté for 3 minutes. Add crushed red pepper, paprika, oregano, and cumin, and sauté for a minute. Add bay leaf and orange mixture and boil for a minute. Add onion mixture, and then shred pork before discarding the bones.

Add the rest of the ingredients and cook as needed.

Serve and enjoy!

Slow-Cooked Chicken with Oregano, Grape Tomatoes, and Orzo

Prep: 20 minutes
Cook: 2 to 4 hours

Ingredients:
Snipped fresh oregano
1 Tbsp grated Parmesan Cheese
2 Tbsp lemon juice
1 tsp lemon peel, shredded finely
1 ½ cups cooked orzo pasta
2 cups grape tomatoes
1 10 oz pack frozen spinach, thawed and chopped
3 garlic cloves, minced
1 14 ½ oz can reduced-sodium chicken broth
1 Tbsp olive oil
4 8 oz boneless and skinless chicken breasts
1/8 tsp ground black pepper
¼ tsp salt
1 tsp dried parsley, crushed
1 tsp dried basil, crushed
1 tsp dried oregano, crushed

Instructions:

Combine parsley, basil, oregano, salt, and pepper in a bowl and then sprinkle over the chicken. Cook chicken in a large skillet until brown or for at least 6 minutes and then remove from heat.

Combine broth, chicken, and garlic in the bottom of the slow-cooker. Top with tomatoes and add spinach. Cover and cook for at least 2 to 4 hours.

Take the chicken away from the cooker. Cover, and keep warm and then transfer into a large bowl using slotted spoon. Add cooked pasta, lemon juice, and lemon peel and then serve with the pasta mixture.

Garnish with fresh oregano and cheese.

Pulled Pork and Butternut Squash Tacos

Prep: 15 minutes
Cook: 7 hours, 40 minutes

Ingredients:
2 Tbsp Jalapeno Red Wine Vinegar
½ cup orange juice
2 tsp minced garlic
1 onion, chopped coarsely
 2 Tbsp adobo sauce
2/3 canned chipotle in adobo sauce
1 Tbsp olive oil
1 tsp ground cinnamon
1 tsp ground cumin
1 tsp black pepper
2 tsp kosher salt, divided
2 lbs boneless pork loin roast
3 lbs butternut squash, cut into bite-size chunks
Corn tortillas, feta cheese, lime wedges (for serving)

Instructions:

Place the squash in the bottom of the slow-cooker and add some salt.

Season pork with pepper and remaining salt and then add cinnamon, cumin, adobo sauce, chipotle chilis, and olive oil and make sure to rub these all over the meat. Place garlic and onion on top and then add red wine vinegar and orange.

Cover and cook for around 6 to 8 hours or until meat is cooked thoroughly and tender. Shred the pork and place in a large bowl before removing onions and squash. Toss with pork to combine.

Microwave the tortillas and place what you have made inside.

Serve and enjoy!

Slow-Cooked Chocolate Cherry Lava Cake

Prep: 15 minutes
Cook: 3 hours

Ingredients:
2 cups semi-sweet chocolate chips
1 cup instant chocolate pudding mix
2 cups cold 2% milk
1/3 cup canola oil
3 large eggs
1 2/3 cup water
1 pack devil's food cake mix (regular size)

Instructions:
Combine cake mix, eggs, water, and oil in a bowl and then beat on low for at least 30 seconds.

Continue beating cake mix in medium for at least 2 minutes and then transfer into 4 quart slow-cooker.

Whisk pudding mix and milk in a bowl for 2 minutes and let stand until soft-set. Spoon over cake batter and add chocolate chips on top and cook for 3 to 4 hour hours, or until moist.

Serve warm and enjoy!

Slow-Cooked Special Poached Salmon

Prep: 10 minutes
Cook: 1 to 1 ½ hour

Ingredients:
Kosher salt and freshly ground black pepper
2 lbs salmon fillets, skin-on
1 tsp kosher salt
1 tsp black peppercorns
5 to 6 sprigs of fresh herbs of your choice
1 bay leaf
1 shallot, sliced thinly
1 lemon, sliced thinly
1 cup dry white wine
2 cups water

Instructions:
Combine shallots, water, lemon, wine, peppercorns, herbs, bay leaf and salt together in the slow-cooker and cook for at least 30 minutes on high.
Use salt and pepper to season salmon with before placing skin-side down on the slow-cooker. Cover until salmon is opaque and flaky and cook for 45 minutes to 1 hour.
Serve drizzled with olive oil and fresh lemon juice.
Serve and enjoy!

Click here http://amzn.to/1U7azgb to leave a review for this book on Amazon! Don't forget to like Daniel Fast Slow Cooker Meals! LIKE US ON FACEBOOK

https://www.facebook.com/DanielFastRecipes/

To purchase the next book in this series: "Slow Cooking for Two: Best Simple and Deliciously Healthy Recipes Updated for 2016 ", click HERE http://amzn.to/1TBsMna

www.ingramcontent.com/pod-product-compliance
Lightning Source LLC
Chambersburg PA
CBHW061159040426
42445CB00013B/1733

9 780996 070744